WILD IS THE HEART

Wild is the Heart

ALEX WÜRFEL

Independently Published

Wild is the Heart is a collection of aphorisms, epigrams and poetry inspired by the waves of life, divided into four parts: love, life, lovers, ebb and flow.

CONTENTS

~ May you live in love ~
May you own your power
May you subdue your ego
and love yourself enough
to follow your wild heart

AW

L-O-V-E

It's no secret that love starts with you.

Alex Würfel

Open your mind
for love is a free bird
that cannot thrive in a cage.

Alex Würfel

Live with an expansive mind
and a heart prolific in love.

Alex Würfel

Here & Now

Love exists in priceless moments

and the mundane everyday moments

converted into precious memories

born out of being present

living in the love vibration

Alex Würfel

Priceless Moments

Sometimes a moment feels so magical to me,
I already miss it even before it has passed.

Alex Würfel

Kindness

Being humane
is the most beautiful sign
of a human being being human.

Alex Würfel

Black Rock City

A magical place where love is enough
to complete the picture because people
leave their egos at the border.

Alex Würfel

Those who don't surrender to love
will remain drifters in life.

Alex Würfel

Love is the only way to get meaningfully far in life.

Alex Würfel

L⚡FE

Life isn't perfect, but it is priceless.

Alex Würfel

Starry Nights

Starry nights are for
dreamers and creative spirits
the ones who count blessings
and turn feelings into art

Starry nights are for
rock bottom moments
shining solace
on extra dark nights

Starry nights are for
synthwave vibes and late night drives
bike ride adventures into the deep playa
lovers lying in a hammock together
chilled beach bonfire moments
making magical memories
with your tribe

Starry nights are for every soul
to feel connected to the Universe
to be present
to exude love
to vibrate higher

Alex Würfel

Waves of Life

Perhaps in life there will be
moments of extreme happiness,
you will feel like you are on
a never ending magic carpet ride
flying high through cloud 9.

In such moments count your blessings.

Other times,
life will throw curve balls at you
that may contain moments of
darkness, struggle and pain.

In such moments count your blessings.

Each tide high or low, contains a life lesson.
To feel fulfilled, live in gratitude.

When all is said and done,
count your blessings because life is a blessing
and in the end all that will remain are the memories.

Alex Würfel

The existence of contrast teaches us mortals
not to take our blessings for granted.

Alex Würfel

If it's not valuable to you, let it go.
If it's important to you, don't give up.
If it's beyond your control, let it be.

Alex Würfel

Tick-tock, wake up!
Smile and thank God for today.
What will you do with all this precious time?

Alex Würfel

It's pleasant to daydream,
but how sweet it is to be a dream-doer.

Alex Würfel

If you are rich in love,
almost anything is possible.

Alex Würfel

The antidote to stagnation is
refusing to give up on yourself.

Alex Würfel

Ignoring your heart may work for a while,
but in the end suppressed desires
only burn stronger.

Alex Würfel

If not now, then when?
is a question you should
ask yourself, then act now.

Alex Würfel

Seeking approval disempowers you;
approving of yourself empowers you.

Alex Würfel

Believing in yourself is the only way
to activate your magic.

Alex Würfel

If you wholeheartedly believe in someone and their abilities, but they don't believe in you, dethrone them from your life.

Alex Würfel

In lone wolf mode,
you call the shots.

Alex Würfel

Discipline

The momentary thrill
of instant pleasure is nice,
but the rich satisfaction one
experiences from the rewards of
delayed gratification is simply the best.

Alex Würfel

Results

Half-hearted attempts or nothing at all
will always amount to mediocrity.
Going above and beyond will
almost always amount
to exceptionality.

Alex Würfel

Arriving at your version of success as slow as a turtle
is as good as arriving as fast as a lizard as opposed to
just giving up when the going gets tough,
or not even trying at all.

Alex Würfel

Witch and *wizard* are merely witty synonyms
for owning one's power.

Alex Würfel

Train your head, but don't tame your heart.

Alex Würfel

No matter how old you are,

never lose touch with the kid in you;

always make time for play.

Alex Würfel

The true winners in life are the ones who live in love:
the free spirits, the magic makers, and the lovers,
those who follow their wild hearts.

Alex Würfel

LOVERS

Brave are the lovers
who choose each other everyday.

Alex Würfel

In Sync

Sometimes people outgrow each other in relationships,
other times we simply need to grow individually first.

Alex Würfel

Win-Win

The more you love yourself,
the deeper your love
for each other
can grow.

Alex Würfel

On the subject of love,
time and distance are meaningless.

Alex Würfel

When All Is Done And Not Said

Lovers on the rocks, think thrice.
If you allow your egos to bypass love,
remember the heart is stubborn too,
it doesn't let go of who it loves.

When all is done and not said,
do your hearts still search
for each other?

Alex Würfel

Crazy Little Thing Called Love

It's not about being with somebody
you can't live without because in reality
people can actually live without each other.
It's about being with the only person
your heart feels lost without.

Alex Würfel

That's Amore

lose and find yourself in wild romance
discover the yin to your yang in a person
whose soul syncs with yours
who drives you crazy
in the best way
and at times
drives you up
the wall too
because after all

there is no such thing as a perfect partner,
but if it is true love they will be worth it all.

Alex Würfel

When I see a full moon,

sunrise and sunset,

I think of you.

Alex Würfel

I can't deny our hearts are connected
and the way our souls groove together
feels like home.

Alex Würfel

~ sun, sea and silliness ~
there's something about
the way we laugh and play.
we go together like June & July,
sunshine flowing through our veins.

Alex Würfel

vibing high into the magic of the night
moon child grooving together
dancing our way into sunrise
synchronised howling
laughing & loving
celebrating life

that's the way we roll!

Alex Würfel

Our hellos are always the sweetest.

Alex Würfel

RedWineMoments™

A bottle of red
you and I
a party for two

Love is a wonderful cause
I adore celebrating with you

Cheers to love
Cheers to us
Cheers to life

Alex Würfel

Baba Cuddles

In each other's arms,
the feeling is priceless.

Alex Würfel

In my arms his ego checks out and so does mine,
as this is the man I fell in love with.

Alex Würfel

Lovers' Farewell
(Lockdown Edition)

"Don't you dare cry baba,
we'll be together again
when this is all over."

From a place of wholeness,
our souls celebrate each other.

Alex Würfel

No Less

If a lover claims to love you & care about you,
but contradictory behaviour speaks louder,
despite how deeply you love this person
and even if it hurts profusely,
don't seek, chase or beg for
their attention & energy,
do nothing.

Sweet words on their own become superfluous,
for love is a verb and actions reigns supreme.

As the saying goes,
The best apology is changed behaviour.
Accept no less, otherwise walk away in silence.

Alex Würfel

Accept nothing less than solid love for each other.

Alex Würfel

The Lovers

living in the here and now ~ accepting the ebb and flow
both expressing yourself completely and connecting deeply
thriving independently and co-creating a shared vision
celebrating life and overcoming life's curve balls
being each other's anchor
learning lessons and counting blessings
inevitably changing and ever-growing
riding the waves of life together
for as long as you both love each other

Alex Würfel

"Cara Mia" ♡ *"Mon Cher"*

Imagine a Gomez & Morticia kind of love
merged with your inner child's best friend

exploring wild and free

sharing full moons, sunrises and sunsets,
being professional cuddlers till the very end.

Alex Würfel

EBB & FLOW

Whichever way the dice rolls in life,
always be a tough cookie with a soft centre.
Use your vulnerability to empower yourself.

Alex Würfel

Never Give Up

When life throws you into the deep end:
Be kind to yourself, tough love yourself up.
Use your pain positively, you are unstoppable.

Alex Würfel

Be like a wildflower,
bloom hardcore against all odds.

Alex Würfel

On the darkest of nights
when there is no moonlight
or shining stars to be seen,
may your heart never fail
to feel the light.

Alex Würfel

No material object,
no amount of money,
no temporary void filler
ever cures the pain a hurt heart carries.

Love is truly the only healer.

Alex Würfel

The egoic mind is like a gatekeeper
that stands between you and happiness.

Alex Würfel

Be gentle with the dragon that is your ego,
let your words be the sword,
slay it with kindness.

Alex Würfel

Perchance you are
out of sync with life,
feel-within-seek-the-lesson.

Alex Würfel

With an open mind,
confusion can turn into
clarity and peace.

Alex Würfel

Oh darling, let it be.
C'est la vie, oui?

Alex Würfel

When you heal inside,
you raise your vibration
and become magnetic.

Alex Würfel

Woman

A woman is capable of
being both a damsel in distress
and the heroine of her own life,
but never at the same time.

Alex Würfel

Lioness Heart

In her weakest moments,
her heart always guides her
back to her throne.

Alex Würfel

If one can thrive in lone wolf mode,
imagine how far one can go
with one's wolf pack.

Alex Würfel

Solitude and human connection
are both core contributors
to our happiness.

Create your own groovy balance.

Alex Würfel

May we all hone one's magic
and share it with others.

Alex Würfel

This Is Your Life

Get out of your own way and don't take

anybody else's life prescription as your path.

Trust the compass of your wild heart.

Alex Würfel

Instagram
@SASHA.DICE